Gallery Books
Editor Peter Fallon

THE TRAVELS OF SORROW

Dermot Healy

THE TRAVELS
OF SORROW

Edited by Peter Fallon

Gallery Books

The Travels of Sorrow
is first published
simultaneously in paperback
and in a clothbound edition
on 24 April 2015.

The Gallery Press
Loughcrew
Oldcastle
County Meath
Ireland

www.gallerypress.com

ISBN 978 1 85235 641 5 *paperback*
     978 1 85235 642 2 *clothbound*

A CIP catalogue record for this book
is available from the British Library.

The Travels of Sorrow receives financial assistance
from the Arts Council.

Contents

The Travels of Sorrow *page* 11
All the Rumours 13
As You Get Older 14
The Many Wonders of John Conway 15
The Souls 16
The Plough 18
Fetch! 19
October Winds 20
Dry Eyes 22
The Flight 24
En Route to Washington 26
The Tickles of Mating 28
Above the Ancestors 29
The Wife of the Moon 30
The Quick Slow Boat 31
The Long Stretch 32
The Soul Flew from the Tree 33
Friend 34
Songs for Digging 36
The Mirror 38
Out There 43
The Freedom Tree 44
Parsley 45
The Off-button 46
The Word for Lust 48
The Birds I Know 49
The Sentinel 50
Trees in April 51
The Whispering Shells 52
The Fossils of Coral 54
The Night Light 56
The Last of Our Name 57
'I have what I wanted . . .' 64
From the Back Row 65
It Will Happen 66
The Pillow Is On Fire 67

That Cottage 68
The Clouds 69
Prayer for Hisham 70

Editor's Note

Prior to his death on 29 June 2014 Dermot and I had been talking about what would be his fifth collection. I have shaped this book out of the draft manuscript he sent to me and out of the poems he wrote in the months afterwards. I pay special thanks to Dermot's widow, Helen Gillard, for her help and trust in the preparation of *The Travels of Sorrow*.

'The Whispering Shells' reprises, and condenses, a poem of the same name, 'for Inor', in *The Reed Bed* (2001).

Acknowledgments are due to *The Irish Times* (Gerard Smyth), *Poetry Ireland Review* (Vona Groarke) and the *Stony Thursday Book* (Peter Sirr) where a few of these poems were published first.

Peter Fallon
Loughcrew
March 2015

The Travels of Sorrow

for the McSweeneys

Years ago, one of the two
brothers, Pat Donlon,

who did the cooking in the house
in a long apron to below the knee,

went into a rage
and took the china

in the house —
the flower vase,

the milk jug,
the big plates —

and threw them
onto the rocks

on the beach.
Years later,

as I built up
a wall of stone

against the sea,
I began to find

here a handle,
there a small flower,

set in delph.
And they were all

the one style
of porcelain

that came with the house.
A thousand, thousand

high tides
have been and gone

and, with a terrible
sadness,

these broken remains
of an old argument on the alt

are coming in
amongst the gravel,

petals from the dresser
and the mantelpiece,

the little fractures
of despair —

shouting, I've had enough!
Take it, take it all! —

are gathering
in the surf.

For years they've been going out
and in with the tide.

Sorrow never travels
far from home.

All the Rumours

All the rumours ended
when the drowned man rose
in the reeds at Rosses.
At last the dog left the spot

and came home shaking,
then went to the house
of a friend of his master
and lay down.

The only true witness
to what had really happened,
he shed hair on the mat
and ate the leavings

of their first breakfast together.

As You Get Older

As you get older
and the pen begins to run out

you begin — without thinking —
to thank the god

you do not believe in.
It's the man

who does not believe
believes most

by saying, over and over,
in a repetitive prayer,

I do not believe,
I do not believe in anything out there.

So when you
start

cursing the god that does not exist
and the pen fills with anger

that's when
faith

and tyranny
begin.

The Many Wonders of John Conway

Listen to this
and remember it always.

John Conway
often told me over the years

these are the wonders
of Maugherow —

A blanket to fill
the bed of the ocean,

a boot to fit
the foot of the mountain,

a jennet's foal,
a square arsehole,

and the tops of the rushes green.

The Souls

1

On the way to a funeral
in Cavan
a crow flew into the windscreen.

On the way to another funeral
in Cavan
a rabbit went under the wheel.

Listen! I heard souls shoot up
with a thump
straight to heaven,

then I sat in the seat
wondering what was coming
on the next straight stretch.

2

It seems the men and women
I've grown up with
have sprouted wings

or turned into hares —
for a split second —
at the final reckoning.

So I'm going to no more
funerals in Cavan.
Soon there won't be a bird

or a badger left alive in the country.
And if you happen
to be coming over the Curlews

and kill a ferret,
turn back, friend, the chances are
you'll meet my hearse.

The Plough

The new plough in the sky
has moved to the sea side
of the house

to dig a white furrow
through the long acres of clouds
and star nests in the sky.

The old plough of the earth
has come to rest
at the gable,

to question the heavens,
with feet
and ribcage gone skeletal.

There the symbol sits rusting
under its new coat of blue
while the shape it once threw

moves on
along the lazy beds of the constellations,
like a letter in an old alphabet

whose sound is lost
to the tongue;
till, at daybreak, the work of the metaphor

is done.

Fetch!

If you want
to break a dog's heart
throw a stone

into the sea.

October Winds

for Helen, in memory of Bert

When you stood mouthing the hymns
in the school choir
you sang harder than all the rest.

When the nuns put
the girls that were out of tune into the organ loft
or onto the stage of the Town Hall

to sing 'October Winds'
you entered the world of mime,
to sing, without singing, and still keep time.

It must have been tough to shape the lips
and make a face like an angel
and still stay silent

as the singers entered the chant,
heads to the side, the hymn sheet
folded at a slant.

Love, silence is the hardest song to sing.
It has more notes than sound
and is only heard years later

as you hum in your head
the words for sorrow
as you will tomorrow

that, like the words of those songs,
will never be heard,
but for the echo that travels

through all of our heads
into the silence
of words that never got said.

Dry Eyes

in memory of Clifford

1

When I got the dry eye
the cat was blamed
for all the years

she had spent
sitting on my shoulder
or on the arm of the chair.

She was put outside
and not let in again.
Every evening

she tore the sea salt
off the windows
with her claws

to watch us within.
She died outside,
in the kennel, aged nineteen.

2

Neither the dog
nor the other cat
ever entered

the kennel again.
I broke it asunder
for firewood.

But she was not to blame
for whatever it was
still burns my iris;

my dry eyes continued
after her death
except on the day

I buried her.

The Flight

The moon sailed in on the ebb,
jib sail aloft,

and filling fast
chased through

the dark swirling sky,
across the troughs,

as if there were many
to come after her;

then on her side
she stopped

to dock
a moment in a pool,

then swung above
my trousers on the line,

and went beyond the vests
and shirts and turf,

the tin rooves
and lewing cows,

till, with seacloud trailing
in her wake,

at the alt
she took one last look.

We were in the house, TV on,
when she baled light

onto the yellow strand
and, lightened of her load,

went on.

En Route to Washington

I'm gonna
have to move
this shit
to have
a piss,

said a voice over my shoulder
after we took off from Shannon
where all the blinds were pulled.

A mist
is an exhalation
of breath
above potato furrows
made of clouds
and May bushes.

On the horizon they build up into an angel's head
who is quiet now but soon will rage;
just wait a while, and turn another page.

The real angel
lives in the mist
beyond belief,
he can kill
himself,
and us.

In the cockpit the final call to God
was Muslim, down the aisles
the last plea was mainly Christian,

as both tribes
balanced
in the air

for the final descent,
face-down in the direction
their prayers were sent.

The Tickles of Mating

for Jack Donlon

The cicadas of Ecuador
start the buzz by beating
their timbals
together in time;

the fireflies
do it by synchronizing
the sparks
in the dark;

the zigzags of Crete
begin by piping
a sac
under their wings,

while the snipe of Finea
whisk the song
out of the feathers
in their tail:

God bless the sky goat.
I've heard him
chase through the mists
and halos over Jack's;

and I've seen the flies
shepherd the stars
at last into flocks
in the Valley of the Volcanoes.

Above the Ancestors

Here's the geese,
there's the curlew.

Now I can turn
the radio on.

Let in
the swan,

and hear
from what direction

the past
is coming from.

The Wife of the Moon

The full moon has wanted the house
for years. When I came here first
I used to hear it heaving at the door
like a husband barred from home.

Out to sea it sat paddling on top of every swell.
I could feel it under my feet,
the January moon, grounding
down the rocks. Now a few years on he's still there

pounding at the foundations.
Oh, but I've become a veteran
of the fierce moon, I no longer move
rocks to placate him, I've grown

complacent, hide out by the hearth,
tuck into wine, watch hours of TV,
then comes a night when
again I encounter the wide light

of that old master riding out
on the old sea and coming
in on the new, searching the dark
for just one perfect opening.

The Quick Slow Boat

The wind approaching
   like a dog in a hurry.

Take everything in,
   the stool

and the cot.
   It's coming into November.

Time to get ready
   to forget

to remember.
   Look out at that boat,

the fierce wave
   on the prow.

I'd risk heresy,
   I would.

Go now.
   Beside the uncertainties

in black veils
   stand the certainties.

Christ! King!
   Go to the devil

and settle that row
   not of our making!

The Long Stretch

for Liam O'Flynn

He sits with the pipes
across his knees,
ready to begin
the long stretch.
The pad for stop
opens like a muscle.
The screech goes through the school.
Then, as he winds his way down
along the keys
to find the note for grief,
he is suddenly at the back
of a lone field
with a scythe up
high to his left,
ready to cut
the leaf
of the buttercup,
with always one foot
propped forward,
keeping
time.

The Soul Flew from the Tree

The soul flew from the tree.
It went underground.

The curlew's cry
was a fugue in the fog.

All winter the tree
stood in the dark

soulless, till slowly
the branches went light

with the weight
of man.

Then the first
soul sang,

'Oh, the little there is
made many!

'Sickness is a cat
pulled through a sock!

'Oh, the little there is
made many!'

as the first blues
climbed the wild hollyhock.

Friend

in memory of Thady and John

John might take the Long Squares,
Thady the New Road.
They might not speak in the Long Hall
but Thady'd knock and call on his way,
'Are you there?' 'I am, I am.
I'm not so bad.' One night

there was no answering shout.
'No sign of Moffit,'
Thady said from the corner of the bar.
He drank and then he turned in his long coat
and, head down, said again, 'There's no Moffit
below.' So we got into the car

and tipped into the house
and found John in his bed,
dressed as if he were taking a nap.
Thady said: 'He's dead.'
He tightened his hands. 'Without John
there's no sense in going on.

Let's go.' A month later Thady said,
'Can we stop for a whiskey on the way?'
when the ambulance came to his door.
'We will,' promised the driver.
'Right.' Thady stood to get up,
then shook, and fell to the floor.

Dead. Now the two houses
sit dark, looking towards each other
across a small road.
One ghost is waiting for the other to call.

We drive by, seeing in front of our eyes
what we do not believe in.

At the funerals the mourning
was silent, like a wound
not healed; some of the same spades
went into the same earth
and you felt the men were burying
the same man twice.

Few wept, they joked
but there was a silence —
a long silence over the promise
that was kept. I did not believe
Thady when he declared
his fate. Nor did I think

we'd find John dead
the night we entered his gate.
As I looked at him
I swore that he slept.
I heard Thady speak behind me,
I heard what he said,

but I never knew
the truth of his words
till long after he was dead.
Now I know another meaning
of that word *friend*.
It means who will follow you
when it comes to the end.

Songs for Digging

for Tess and Josie

1

With the first shovelful
of earth

tossed
over your shoulder

it's '*Hosanna,
Hosanna*

in the highest'
you hum

as you curse
the blasted scutch

and dig
into the cursed bind.

2

When the spade
strikes rock

and the pain
travels up the arm

into the brain
with a jolt

it's time for
'Who put

my Granny off the bus'
as you thumb

up the road
towards home.

3

Evening.
The yard skims

with swallows.
There's only

a few hours to go.
'On top

of Old Smokey,
all covered with snow'

is for laying
the flag stones

up to the new door.

The Mirror

1

They say
that if you put a mirror

in front of a baby
he will just point at it —

Look at that other person,
that fellow

over there!
See him, the finger says,

Look! Who is he?
But at eighteen months

he'll peer into the mirror
and slowly touch his face

and see it's himself
he's been laughing at.

And that's when
speech starts —

after that first
laughter.

When you recognize yourself
in the mirror

and see at last that the clown
is yourself

then the words
for others begin.

2

But the mirror can
bring silence too.

There was
a long silence

between two babies
that were joined at birth,

then separated
and placed in different beds

till
the stitches set;

and they cried
constantly,

wanting
the other back

till a mirror was put
into each cot

and immediately
they quietened down.

3

They looked at
the familiar face

in front
of them

in great wonder
and saw the one

they missed
for a long

uninterrupted
instant:

and at last
the two slept

thinking
the other was there

at just
a touch away.

4

The mirrors
were removed

when the scars
healed enough

for them to be put
facing each other

in the one bed.
And again

came that long
questioning

look.
Everything stopped.

They didn't move a muscle
as they took the other in,

and then came a near smile
of recognition;

and something else
crossed the face

that did not happen
in the mirror —

the faint smiling trace
of loss appeared.

5

Now that they were together
another separation

began,
longer than all the rest.

You will be taken from me,
the eyes said,

but the silence
was never broken.

They aged a little
in their twin beds

as they studied
the life in the years ahead

without a word
being spoken.

Out There

And in a neighbour's window
a tall bowl of tall flowers
stands like a woman

with her hands
squeezed round her hips,
shoulders aslant

and head tilted forward,
as she studies what's happening
out there today.

The Freedom Tree

The rings thinned in the tree
as the drought grew.
All that summer long the ring
on your marriage finger

loosened till you lost it
in a snowdrift in the Rockies.
But when the weather softened
the ring grew again wide behind the bark.

In a stream below the tall poplars
the vow glistened.
We bought another, and woke
years later to thunder in the dark.

I'll be buried beside him,
you said to the girl in the back.
Now it's not one of us will die,
but two, alone, and yet,

with each death
the closer we grew,
the greater the bondage
the greater the freedom

we knew.

Parsley

In the dark of the garden
is the parsley — a bare stalk
covered in sea salt,
but above the root
there's a brief spray of leaf
shooting up through the cold
toward the year to come,
ready again to begin
the endless talk
of children —
those children you left
when they were young,
and will leave you
when they grow old.
I'm young. Take me up!
Gather me into your arms.
I have the spit of rain on my breath.
The fern caps are tossing.

The Off-button

I looked out
but all I could see
was myself
at the window

blocking the light.
Earlier I saw
the TV on
in a sudden spot

of rain. The programmes
had changed. Someone
had pressed
in

the off-button.
I'm getting
to the point
of no return.

When the skiers
flap their wings
I know
it's called sport;

when the dead
in a hand-held video
are lying in a square
I know it means war.

The ordinary
I suddenly understand
needs to go abroad.
And the stranger

needs to come home.
I got this advice
as moonlight
whitened the stones.

The Word for Lust

The word for lust is good,
a nice pistol shot
across the tongue,

but not as good
as the word
for love

which must have been formed
when the top teeth
grazed

the bottom lip
of some linguist
who took a break

to breathe out
after the honk
in the cave

happily adding —
with a toss of the head
and a cursory wave

to the ancestors —
more pain
to the language.

The Birds I Know

In the ditch
the grasses collect in families
while the thin conductor, fast asleep,
waves, ready to begin again

in a light wind
as the sheep
cross the field
in a wandering line,

while the birds I know
grow less
as their numbers
multiply

round a bare tree trunk
with the apron strings of ivy
tied at the waist
and feet.

The Sentinel

The robin likes to stand guard
as you work. You're in here
for life, it seems; the stones
you're carrying to the ditch
turn into tombs you'll be buried
under one day. If you look up
she looks away, one wing to the side
like a dismissal by a lady's fan —
Less of the common talk, please,
but pray, you simpleton, if you must!
Half the time she sings unknownst
to me as I pull at weeds
down on my knees
at Riogs, the last days of March,
the first of April. The clout
of cold wind is waiting in the wings.
I stand to get my breath
and get light in the head.
On the top of the bush,
with her heart out,
my sentinel sings.

Trees in April

The trees in Strandhill
collect in kimonos
and broad hats
to greet the wind.

At Lissadell
they stand leafless
and skeletal
without a whisper.

The Whispering Shells

The tide mark in March
is a whispering line of shells

that have come in, ears down,
onto the beach

and there they chatter
among the sandflies

so that if you would live on
you must listen

and in each you can hear
the tiny sound of your own shrill voice

looking for a break
in the weather,

calling out to your fellows
and their awesome replies

as you paddled the deep
waters of the unnamed,

and drew closer
through the slough

of teeming sandflies
to dock

at this strange
drunken coast

where the first thing
each man heard

was his own
whispering shell.

The Fossils of Coral

for Eilish, in memory of David Slack

1

After a storm
I collected the coral stones
I'd promised him,

each filled
with a tropical sea,
and the scrawl and dint of time.

As I entered the room he told me
that the robin on the sill
had turned into an autumn leaf.

Then David took the fossils
in both of his hands
and balanced them

and said:
'This one is Darwin
and this one is the Bible.'

He weighed them again
in his hospital bed,
moving them

from one hand to the other
and nodded:
'I'm keeping an open mind.'

2

Weeks later
he went cheerfully into oblivion
leaving the question behind.

At the funeral Mass
among the gifts brought to the altar
were the two fossils of coral

and a set of chess men.
From morning to night
he used replay old games

in the kitchen, moving the knights
and pawns
around in his head,

till he made the final move
the last time
he saw his father.

David was wheeled out from the hospice.
His father was wheeled in from the car at the gate.
They sat outside the County Home.

Seamus Slack was approaching ninety.
He looked over at his son
who was less than half his age.

David, knowing he'd die first,
took a drag of a fag, leaned over and tapped
his father's arm, and said:

'Checkmate!'

The Night Light

One evening,
years before he died,

Johnny Conway said,
'You must have had a late night.

'Me saw your outside light on
this morning in the dark.'

'You must have been
out early,' I replied.

'Me was. At early feeding.'
Years later his words

come back —
the way he nodded,

the way he smiled,
The 'I' that was a word

he never said —
when, just before bed,

I stepped out the door
by orders

of my lost guide
to check the night light,

and all was dark
until his voice

suddenly lit up
the yard.

The Last of Our Name

She woke me up
demanding that
all the barriers
I had erected

over the years
to preserve myself
be removed at once:
Are you listening!

The argument
can start
at any hour,
always the same story.

He wants me out,
right now,
she wants the land
back, he wants the bent,

the flags, the anemone,
the flax is rightly his.
Even the abandoned car
must go.

And to hell with
the fucking books!
Take them with you.
What do I care!

Then she relents,
his humour eases,
we're back where
we started;

till some slight
out there in her past
sends him into a fury:
the door slams shut;

she's gone, moved
out for days
and stays,
unrepentant,

with distant relations
to vent her spleen,
then back again
on the easing tide

from another continent
with the anger spent;
and now is all luxuriant
and whispering.

But I know
what's coming —
that flood
at first light

will start the next row
behind windows
closed by
inches of salt.

Outside all day a spray
of silent gravel rises
and in come the suds
and the thump of the swell,

with the moon in the third
on her hunkers,
digging down into
the night.

The worst is at
the filling in of the moon
when the blame
comes in from the North West

and, empty-headed,
the plants scream
and shed
their leaves.

Long ago
she gave back the ring,
took the road,
the thrift, the whin,

leaving him with custody
of the children.
It was beautiful
at the beginning,

the rows
brought them out at night
to the head of the alt
to look down below

at the quiet waters.
But the adventure
stopped long ago.
If I look into my heart

I could see it coming
from the very start:
nothing pleased her,
not even the swan

on the small pond.
Even the goose
vexed him.
Nights she pounds

the gable.
Let me in!
Let me in!
Now comes the final demand:

she wants the house
and everything in it.
I've lost my friends.
The ones who are safe

are the worst.
I am cursed.
History and neighbours
are on his side.

They gave evidence
against my defence,
belittled the slopes
of grass,

smirked
at the gabions
until with venom
my rocks were seized

and hurled
to heaven
without the least sound.
The sea did a murder.

Then came the depressions,
the drinking,
the dementia,
the salt tears.

The inspectors agreed:
he is beyond redemption.
Yes, there is no cure
for her fears.

I have no rights,
her case
rests on
a geographical fault

I made all those nights
ago when I moved
into his bed.
My ignorance

was read
out to the court.
He was warned
but she persisted.

She wants me out.
Take your things,
be gone! she screams
at high tide.

Go anywhere,
get out! You will not be missed.
Go inland,
go, back to all your tribe,

to the edge
of that dismal lake
of the mists.
A poor mistress,

a mild master,
without passion
will suit,
even save you.

I say, I won't move.
I will take action,
she promises,
that you will regret.

There is the door.
My patience is spent.
We step out
into the commotion

of that never-
ending ocean
which nightly shouts out
its loud cry

of nothingness.
To go or stay
is to tempt fate.
On the high bank

the marram grass
blows as we wait.
I have the radio on
for him to listen to.

Temper dies down.
We go our own way
about the house
till, some time during the night,

the wind
closes the gate —
the tidings
are bad —

a hundred miles out
the argument has begun
again on the Sea Road
of the Saints.

They sit down
to another last breakfast together.
Hailstones burst like shells
on the galvanize roof.

The dog and the cat
and the horse run for cover.
The old war is rowing in
on the next wave.

'I have what I wanted . . .'

I have what I wanted
but I've given it away.

The slow deluge from the heavens
has the last say

and when it stops
with final drops

I'm back in London
listening to thunder.

From the Back Row

The tied stone
is an angry dog.
The moored boat
travels far in fog.

It Will Happen

Oh, for an orderly system
of mind that arrives
on Saturday afternoons,

after a drive in the mountains.
When I take the time
to mind the clues,

settle into the chair
with memory intact,
all the randomness

peacefully random,
the cows that will die
looking out to sea,

content, and what I will do
now of little import:
it will happen.

Outdoors, a minute ago,
a butterfly blew by
like a sliver of ash.

There's fresh onions
in the earth. The wounds
on the wrist are healing.

The Pillow Is On Fire

The hardest thing
is to wake up
    and find the tears
    on the pillow
        are your own.

Or there's worse, when your hair
catches fire at the hearth
    without your knowing,
    and there's no one there
        to douse it.

So remember, leman,
what has to be done — throw your head
    into the pillow of tears
    to put out
        the flames.

That Cottage

That cottage
one of thousands
and thousands
sitting alone
below the mountains
below the hills
behind the trees
along the lakes
ticks away
like a clock inside my head;
the sound of the alarm;
the kettle boiling;
the man on the stick
at the gate waving;
and the wife out
on the Woman's Road
setting flowers.

Loneliness gathers.
Here we are.

The Clouds

And beneath us, in the clouds,
    my mother's hair goes by,
        till there they are,

all the aged,
    drawing the curtain
        across the sky

Prayer for Hisham

I have no prayer,
only what I see.
The words I say
were made up by others

to speak for me.
If I could I would
put an end to prayer
so that I myself

might hear
how close the distant is
to what sits
so near;

then the echo
might reach the ear
of some other
woken by

the unspoken;
and we might speak
over the centuries
without moving

our lips,
in the silence
that was given away
by the silent

as a gift.